The Video Game Truck Business:

Is The Niche Service Business For Me?

Lee Sulima

Copyright © 2016 Lee Sulima

All rights reserved.

ISBN: 1541218698
ISBN-13: 978-1541218697

INTRO

Hello hello everyone this is **"Lee the videogame truck guy"** and first and foremost I would like to thank you for taking the time to pick up this book, it means a lot to me.

A little bit about myself, originally, I immigrated to the United States from the Soviet Union after it fell apart, I am very grateful and thankful that I live in this amazing country. GO USA GO! It is because I am here that I am able to do what I do and that is, run this amazing niche service business. I would also like to thank my team who works relentlessly, my mother who taught me the value of hard work and my beautiful wife who puts up with me ☺

When I started, without knowing any better I went directly into one of the most saturated markets in the nation and that is the Los Angeles area. That was definitely one of the factors that forced me to move my butt very fast. However, the chances are that there are a few to none video game trucks where you are. I can tell you for sure Los Angeles is one of the most heavily competitive video game truck areas in the nation. Most other parts of the nation still don't even know what the video game truck is!

Let me rephrase that whole paragraph, there is an insane amount of potential in this business in most parts of the country.

Anyhow, I was stuck at a job that I hated and it was driving me crazy. Overworked, underpaid and suffering medical related issues I started researching businesses and found the niche, a mobile kids service business with video games.

I will admit, even though I researched the business I was bias when pulling the trigger on it because video games was something I always loved.

So, I went on "the google" picked up the phone, called a company that looked like what I was looking for and then about a week later I had my video game trailer. I drove it back from the East Coast to the West Coast with a big grin on my face.

Originally when I started, I started with a company called Rolling Video Games. I still own some trailer units from this company because in the starting years I built up the brand very strong in certain geographical locations and it does not make sense to me to part ways. Instead of completely getting away from that brand, I simply kept it and launched my own brand alongside.

I was happy and excited because I was finally going into business for myself. The problem with the whole thing was I had absolutely no idea what I was doing in the beginning so it was definitely a very very hard start for me. There was no educational material at the time on the Internet to learn from. It was also difficult to network because there really weren't that many people who I knew in business and to be honest with you I was afraid to pick up the phone and make contacts to learn from other video game truck owners.

So here I was with my slightly used trailer that I thought was brand-new when I bought it but did not care because I was so excited. With little direction, as to what I was supposed to do but lots of enthusiasm and energy I was ready to take on Los Angeles. Looking a couple of years later I have multiple trailers servicing events and some very awesome employees. Currently my company is servicing the Los Angeles area, Orange County area and the Inland Empire. Basically, a big populated chunk of Southern California.

Anyhow, then I asked myself the following question. **What next?**

I said to myself "Lee you can do a much better job and not just servicing events, but also making the units and selling them. **Why?** Because current models are not adaptable or practical enough to fit into the future of gaming.

You see, I'm not lucky or fortunate enough to have a lot of talent, but the two things I do know how to do is reverse engineer things and work very long hours until there is a positive result. Those are pretty much the only two things I think I'm good at. Any time there is a problem that I encounter in business, the first thing I do is look at all the top individuals or companies in my problem area, learn from them, and put in the time to produce a positive result.

One of the first services I offered to others was training people from all around the country who wanted hands on experience in the business. I figured that I could make an extra $1500 bucks over the weekends and show potential clients the ropes. It was a three-day learning event were a client could ask me anything business related and shadow me on three work days. It was great meeting people from Texas, Pennsylvania, Florida etc.... They came from all over the country and that was super awesome.

Some short time later I asked myself the following questions,

Okay, how can I go further? What can I do to really really hit the nail on the head and offer more to others?

That's when I came up with the idea of hey, I'm just gonna start building these things myself and as I build them, I will just expand my own current market and grow locally.
I found an excellent welder, a carpenter, electrician and started to build the units.

Initially it was a good idea, the problem with it was that every time my team and I built a new unit for my company to be used by my company somebody wanted one. So, I started selling them. I sold the first few cheap just because I found it fun to build and learn. While other companies outsource many aspects of construction I'm hands on in the shop. My company had two new trailers and after those two trailers I was never able to build more for my company because every time the third trailer came out someone bought it.

I said to myself "**something is going really right here**" I said to myself "**Lee what can you do to be the next big thing in the industry? What is the future of this business?**" The answer to those questions was virtual reality. Virtual reality is still in its infancy but the demand for it is already climbing.
I started doing more research and realized that VR this is the next big thing, but the old trailers, the standard trailers that are sold nationwide, they are not properly set up for virtual reality. I call those trailers the 1.0 models.
So I said "**Okay, from this point what is it that I need to do

to be able to accommodate virtual reality and the standard video games?"

And that's when the 2.0 unit was born. Ever since then, I have never looked back. Now with the 2.0 unit there is more internal real estate and there are other cool benefits as well.

I made a promise to myself in early 2016, and that was not to just to be another company that goes out and services events, but to be the new industry leader in service, training, support and quality product that is practical, adaptable and easy to use.

Whenever a gentleman or lady picks up a new unit from me I look him or her straight in the eye and shake their hand. Then I say "If you need any help please do not hesitate to call because even though you are in a turnkey business I will provide something for you that no one has ever been able to provide for me, and that is genuine support. I don't want you to just make it, I want you to be successful.

Thank you so much, I hope that this book can be of help to you.

"The value of an idea lies in the using of it."

Thomas Edison

CONTENTS

1	What I Learned From The Mobile Video Game Business	Pg 1
2	The Starting Business Options	Pg 12
3	Getting Started	Pg 23
4	Add on Businesses	Pg 27
5	Marketing 101	Pg 33
6	The Future of the Business	Pg 41
7	Questions To Ask Before You Buy a Used Unit	Pg 43

ACKNOWLEDGMENTS

Thank you to my family, build team and the people who work for me. Each one of you is extremely important to me. Without you, I would not be able to be where I am now. God bless you all. May fortune forever smile upon you.

1 WHAT I LEARNED FROM THE MOBILE VIDEO GAME BUSINESS

This chapter I would like to go over some of the advantages and what I've learned about operating a mobile videogame business.

1) It is a very flexible model
2) This is a perfect start for the new business owner or for someone who is retired
3) It is a niche opportunity that keeps out the fakers
4) You are the indirect center of attention
5) The convenience element
6) You market there, where the businesses is!
7) Referrals, referrals, and more referrals
8) You are driving a huge billboard
9) No spoiling inventory
10) This business can be operated by one person
11) Inexpensive maintenance
12) Flexible hours
13) Training replacement is not as difficult
14) Practical 2.0 units are easy to maintain
15) Low competition in most areas
16) You get to play video games!

17) It is a growing industry
18) Don't have a new game yet but it's out? Go rent it!
19) Networking with other businesses
20) Growing your business and other options.

1) It is a very flexible model

In the past I had the experience of starting up a brick and mortar business. Even though it was very short-lived I learned quite a bit from that experience. I had to apply for permits, I had to go through fire inspection, look at different insurances, city regulations, it was not fun. One of the key advantages for this mobile business is that you do not have to deal with most of these headaches. Basically, once you have your equipment, as long as you know where to park it and you have the proper insurance, you are good to go. Every business has its difficulties but a mobile business as a whole has a lot less providing that you're doing the right one. I believe that a mobile videogame business model is flexible and has a minimum risk. For me, it turned out to be the right business model.

2) This is a perfect start for the new business owner or for someone who is retired

Looking to do something part-time maybe or full time? If you never owned a business before and this is your first, the learning curve isn't as high since it is a turnkey business provided you get the right training. If you are retired and simply looking to supplement some income during the weekends this is also a very good choice. The flexibility is that you set your own hours and so even if you are still working a 9 to 5 job, you can start this business on the side. This is the only business I know that has the ability to adapt to a standard 9 to 5 schedule. This is the only business I know that can be operated only during the weekends if the operator chooses to do so.

3) It is a niche opportunity that keeps out the fakers

Not all niches are created equal and the videogame truck business model niche stands solely on its own. Besides being a unique service entertainment business, I learned that **the amount of money required to get into it is not astronomically high, however, it's just enough to keep out the fakers.** What do I mean by fakers? I mean people who are not serious. You need to have some capital to get into this business. Anyone who starts with us invests 45k to 65k for their unit. This is a reasonable investment for a unit and it's just out of the reach for those who are not serious. For example, it's a lot easier to start a photo booth business for 5 thousand but the return on a photo booth business without a video game truck does not come close. It's easier for someone who is not serious to go into the photo booth business so the competition in that niche is higher. But vice versa, if you offer a video game truck and piggy back a photo booth service as well, now you just crushed the other competitor because you over delivered. You made a good investment.

4) You are the indirect center of attention

Once you start operating this business you will quickly find out that people want to be around you and your business. You are the indirect center of attention because kids love video games and they just can't get enough. When they see you come by their house or by their school or whatever the event is, everyone wants to go inside and play. You will soon get to learn that as you drive by, the kids will be screaming "Game truck! Game truck the videogame truck is here!". Get used to it because it happens almost all the time.

5) The convenience element

One of the biggest pluses about running this business is that it's not just catering to the kids, it's also catering to the parents who pay for the event. Think about it for a moment, why go to a place that's a brick and mortar far and away from the house when the fun can come to the house. The parents don't have to go anywhere, they don't have an extra headache and everyone's having fun right there and then. The convenience element of this business drives this business astronomically high, there is a demand for it. All parents really want to do is provide their children with a safe and fun environment while they themselves do not have to do all of the work. The actual party for the parents is easy because you help them by becoming the babysitter who runs the event for 2 to 4 hours while they sit back, have conversations and glass of wine if they want.

6) You market there, where the businesses is!

Because you are in the mobile service business you can gather data and then go to the location of the business. In the brick-and-mortar you cannot do that, the business has to come to you. So if there are a 100 schools nearby and 100 churches you can go to all of these locations and provide the service on the spot. You do not have to market in one geographical location. You are free to market in the hot areas were the business is good.

7) Referrals, referrals, and more referrals

In this business, you will have anywhere from 10 to 30 kids playing at the same time at any average event. Every one of those children has a birthday. Because this is a low competition niche business and because it is so easy on the parents the referrals are insane. You will be very surprised to find out when your phone rings and someone says **"Hey 2 months ago, you did a birthday party for my son's friend can you do one for us in 2 weeks?"**

8) You are driving a huge billboard

Another very awesome thing about this business is that no matter where you go that eyeballs are always on your trailer with your website and your telephone number. Curiosity is an amazing thing that works in your favor. Even if you are stuck in traffic and not moving very fast, as long as you're pulling your trailer behind you, this large billboard will bring in a ton of business for you. I cannot count the times when someone pulled up to me and called while driving. **"Hey is that you driving that gaming truck? Yah I just checked out the website can I book an event with you?"** So be sure to wear a Bluetooth, it makes talking and driving much easier. And in some states like California the law states that a driver must have a hands-free phone device when driving.

9) No spoiling inventory

Unlike in the food business or other business that have perishables, besides videogames you do not have to really spend money on inventory. Once you by your videogame it is good to go for a very long time unless somebody scratches the game and you have to replace it. In general, your inventory stays with you from the beginning. Proper use of the inventory is key. We have some games that are over 5 years old and they still work without any problems.

10) This business can be operated by one person

The great thing is that when you start in this business, if you are a one-man or a one-woman show you can pull it off. Regardless of how you see this business expanding for you in the future, you can run it without much help provided you have the proper training before you get into it.

11) Inexpensive maintenance

If you take the time to figure out what can go wrong and this is actually something that I teach everyone in my courses, you will eliminate 70% of the things that you will have to pay for out-of-pocket. Okay I know maybe 70% is a little high but if you choose to do certain things yourself like change the oil or tires that's pretty much it. Unless something major happens the maintenance on your trailer is not that expensive. Now the truck that you are pulling the trailer with will have other expenses that you will need to hire somebody if you are not a mechanic, when it comes to the truck I do not do maintenance on it unless it's changing the oil or brakes. Doing the general maintenance yourself will save you anywhere from $50 to $300 dollars. The price depends on where you are in the country.

12) Flexible hours

So you want to work only during the weekends? Great. Many people want to just work during the weekends and have the week off. Nothing wrong with that especially if you're retired. However, if you choose to work all week long you can do that too. Unlike in the brick-and-mortar location where you have to physically be present all the time or you have to have somebody constantly on location, you do not have to do that with this business model. And yes, it is true, you will get back from the business what you put into it. The results will be a direct reflection that comes from the amount of work that you do. **But, you are not chained to it and paralyzed as you are in many other business models.**

13) Training a replacement is not as difficult

I'm well aware of the fact that not everyone can drive a truck and trailer combination, that part is probably the hardest part. Learning how to park is also time consuming for someone who never backed up a trailer before. Everything after that however is fairly easy. You learn what the most popular games are and how to help out kids during some game play. Most of the time the problems are repetitive. Finding the solutions to the problems after a couple parties will make you a pro trouble shooter. If you have to replace yourself and or get a backup driver, it should not take more than couple of weeks to train someone to become a good driver and a great game coach. Personality for the replacement is super important. Think twice before hiring someone with low energy.

14) Practical 2.0 units are easy to maintain

I know I already mentioned that the cost for maintaining the trailer is not that high. One thing I forgot to mention is that there is a big difference between a 1.0 unit and a 2.0 unit which we will cover later. A 2.0 unit is much easier to maintain, it's very practical and that is exactly why we prefer to use the 2.0 unit over the 1.0 unit any day of the week.

15) Low competition in most areas

In this niche business, there are very few hot pockets of

competition around the country. Most of the areas in the United States have big voids to fill with this business niche. That's what makes this business a secret hot niche business that not many are aware of. There is a ton of business out there on the market that is available but it has not yet been tapped.

16) You get to play video games

Okay okay, not everyone likes videogames but I have a passion for video games and I love it when a new video game comes out and I get to sit down and play. Sometimes I bring friends and their kids over and we all test the games out and try to figure out everything about them. It is super fun. So, if you like playing videogames then in your official work time you get to play videogames because you have to know your craft. Spending 5 to 6 hours a day sometimes playing a game is actually part of your job.

17) It is a growing industry

The videogame industry is booming, sales numbers are constantly going up. Entertainment is not going anywhere, videogames are not going anywhere. It is a very stable market with growth. The video game truck business opportunity capitalizes on that market. Most people love video games however they cannot afford to buy all of them. When you do an event, you offer a variety of games that kids and adults love to try out and play. No one has to go out and buy lots of games because you provide all of the games for the event.

18) Don't have a new game yet but it's out? Go rent it!

I do this all the time. I know that when a game comes out I need to test it before I buy five or six copies of that game so what I do is rent 3 copies for a $1.50 and invite 2 friends to play the game alongside. After we play it, I try to figure out if it's going to be a good investment to buy five or six copies of that game. If I am still not sure, I will take one or two rented copies to an event and ask some kids what they think about it. If the reviews are positive, then I go out and buy multiple copies. If the reviews are negative, then I simply do not bother. If a special request comes in for that game once in a million years ill simply rent it again for the event.

19) Networking with other businesses

The great thing about being in this business is that you get to network with other businesses. Pizza shops love to work with us, also other food catering businesses love to work with us. Think about it, sometimes you come out to an event and you already networked with a different business that caters food and they come out with you. Sometimes I do this on a commission basis. The caterers kick back $50 to $100 bucks as a thank you. It's a great package deal! No one has to worry about food or entertainment, everything is provided. Why? Because you took the time to establish a cohesive network. You can also work on a referral basis and not a commission basis as long as both companies provide similar return results.

20) Growing your business and other options.

Later on, in the book I will specifically be talking about how you can grow your business and some of the add-ons that you can do to this business. If you've ever watched any of my YouTube videos I talk about the add ons. However, I cover this topic in more detail later on.

2 The Starting Business Options

6 Video Game Truck Business Models

Getting started may be confusing, know your options!

Chapter 2 is a very important chapter, the reason for it is because in this chapter we look at your options before you get into the business. Options are crucial to understand because they paint a picture for you and allow you to see with more clarity how you are going to operate your business. Knowing what your options are will provide you with an edge in the business. Not all options are one size fits all. Many do not know what their options are and so they jump in on impulse blindly. I hope that I can better assist you in making the right decision as to how you're going to get into this business. *Please please please do not jump in blindly on impulse. Do the due diligence first.*

The Video Game Truck Business: Is It For Me?

1) The mother franchise operation
2) The owner operator franchise with support
3) The owner operator franchise without support
4) The turn key non-franchise operation
5) The do it yourself model
6) The hybrid model of **virtualrealitygametruck.com**

1) The first option is what I call the mother franchise option.

This is a very standard approach that has pluses as well as minuses. Anyone who goes into the mother franchise operation usually does so with the mindset of a business owner not of a contractor. Let me elaborate as to what I mean by a contractor mindset. A contractor is someone who services the business him or herself. It is usually a one-man operation. A mother franchise approach is for someone who is looking to operate the business from the sidelines and not necessarily be the one who runs the operation him or herself the entire time. A Franchise is a system. I personally believe that anyone who has the capital to go into the business and does so from a mother franchise operational point of view is making a good decision, however, to truly get into this business it is my opinion when I say <u>*"it's always best to start as a contractor and work your way up to fully understand all of the ins and outs of the business."*</u>
As you grow from a contractor mindset into a business mindset you will overcome multiple obstacles along the way and become much stronger as you expand your business. As a contractor, you build a bridge from one side to the other. It is much easier to rely on experience down the line as you hire because through the contractor

experience you become an expert and a seasoned business owner.

The mother franchise operation is the second most expensive approach.
You're looking at easily $100,000 plus in starting investment capital and we are talking on the low-end. Get ready to pay a whole lot more.

There will be franchise fees.
Is it a percentage of the profit that you must pay?
Is there a flat fee of some sort that you have to pay too?

Most likely you will pay territorial fees. What happens if you decide to operate your business in more than one territory which is very common in this business? Is that covered in your franchise contract? Do you have to pay more for working an extra area? What if there is plenty of business but another franchisee already laid claim to the area and its hands off for you? This is a very important question because if you operate in a 50 mile radius and there are 20 different territories are you liable to the franchise to pay for 20 different locations of operation?

One thing I do like about the franchise approach is that you will most likely get full quality training. Also, many of the major marketing expenses are already covered due to brand-name recognition. Providing the franchise invested in the brand handsomely.

As you continue doing research or even watch some of my YouTube videos you will come to discover that many franchises use the same approach when it comes to marketing and that is through what's known as the _**pay per click**_ on the Google search engine platform.

So, if you know someone who is a marketing expert or maybe you yourself know how to use the platform, one of the questions that's important to ask is, **is it worth to pay a franchise a lot of money when one of their major marketing strengths is doing paper click advertisement when you yourself can do it or hire someone for a lot less money?**

Sometime a franchise has a call center option. This means that everything is filtered through a call center and then you are simply sent information of what event to do and when to do it. I personally have a difficulty following orders from someone because I used to do it all the time when I worked for another company. For me personally the franchise approach is not something that I see as the most flexible and adaptable approach to the video game truck business market.

With the franchise approach the hands are tied in many aspects. You will have to follow rules in a (mother franchise operation business model). One of the many things I like about running my business is that I am flexible to do what I want to do and I do not have to get approval. Let me make an example as to how flexibility is in your favor when you are not in a franchise like set up.

Let's say for a moment that a church wants to rent your service. That church is on a budget and all they have is $150. They want you to come out for a 70 minute event. You look at the map and realize that they are 3 miles away from your location but outside of your city in the next city over. The party is happening on the Wednesday morning.

You say to yourself "this is great I'm going to go make $150 bucks easy. However, if you are under a franchise operation you might not be able to move on that event or change your pricing nor have the negotiation power because that would then be against franchise rules. Also, if the event is 3 miles away but outside your service territory you may not have the rights to service that event because you did not pay the territory fees. Don't get me wrong, if the franchise if properly set up and marketed, it is not a bad option, however it is very important to research and understand what franchise you are going into. Who are the competitors of the franchise in the area?
What data can the franchise provide to you from specifically the area in which you will operate and not just projections, but actual hard numbers. Is a competitor in the area doing better than the franchise? All excellent questions.

2) The next business model that we will looking at is the "Independent owner operator franchise with support"

Although I highly doubt that something like this exists in the Video Game Truck field at the moment, in theory it does exist so that is why I am going to cover it.
In this model the Independent owner operator is given full extensive training, also there is an established company brand. There has already been some existing marketing set up for this franchise so the brand recognition may be somewhat established and that may help the new business operator.
Usually in this approach, because of the support element to the operator, there will be some sort of franchise fee but it should not be an outrageous one.

3) The next model is the "independent owner operator franchise without support"

This is exactly how I started in the business.
I started with a company called Rolling Video Games. I was very fortunate to start in this model because it forced me to learn a lot and then apply everything that I learned to the business. In this approach, I received about three hours of training total.
I was able to use the company brand. That was a plus.
The problem is that it is a business model that comes without support. You are completely on your own. If you happen to be late on your payment your trailer might not be parked in the location where it should be for long because it will get repossessed. This business approach is a very difficult one because you are responsible for everything. You are the CEO of cleaning the trailer and you are the CEO of negotiating deals all at the same time. Over all the marketing is weak. It helps, but not enough. This model has benefited me when I started because I was in a position of pain and so I had to learn how to do everything fast and hold off on the sleep. If you are one of those people who is looking for complete freedom and doesn't care about difficulties, this might be the option for you. However, do your research because without support, for most people, the freedom will cost valuable time and money they do not have.

4) The next option is the turnkey non-franchise operation.

I believe that this business model thus far, has been one of the most successful.
First of all, in this approach you are a contractor and as covered before a contractor mindset in my opinion allows you to grow into a full business mindset properly through experience.

There are no franchise fees,
There are no territorial fees,
Most of the time you will receive full training.

The downside to this type of business model is that there is very little to no marketing support and at times the buyers are sold on certain products that do not necessarily deliver worthy enough benefits.

You might get some pamphlet or some direction as to how you can market and maybe if you're lucky enough you even get a website with your new trailer.

Support in this system varies the second you drive off the lot. You made your deposit, you signed a financing agreement with another company for financing and now you are on your own. There is absolutely nothing that dictates to the company that sold you the trailer that they are going to help you. Keep in mind that a turnkey nonfranchise operation has much flexibility. Many independent owners stay connected and exchange ideas through forums. **_A support system will help, but it's not a master mind group_**. I will talk about it more later on.

5) The do-it-yourself model

Previously I wrote that the mother franchise operation is the second most expensive way to get started. The do-it-yourself model is the most expensive way to get started and let me tell you why.

Unless you are already a business savvy person and you know how to; build, outsource certain elements of the building process, understand the marketing, SEO, SMM, banking, networking, etc... It will be very difficult for you to do it yourself. Don't get me wrong there are some people that can pull this off but for the most part it is very difficult to accomplish.

One thing to consider in the do-it-yourself model is the amount of time it will take for you to get things moving. If it takes you more than six months to start implementing or just to start building your own unit yourself, you are already at a losing position. Speed of execution is a key element in the do-it-yourself model because you are in the process of constantly reverse engineering and trying to figure out what works and what doesn't work. This takes valuable time. I know this because it took a couple of trailers for me to build in the beginning just to get it down. While you are trying to figure these things out your competitors are already moving, marketing and making money. My suggestion to you is that unless you are truly capable, think twice before moving on this option. We had some do it yourself companies in the LA area who cut corners. Cutting a corner in the build process is not the right thing to do if you want to stand out.

6) The Hybrid Model of VirtualRealityGameTruck.com

The next and final model that will be looking at is the **hybrid model** of the:
virtualrealitygametruck.com
I personally believe without bias that this is the best model to get started with in the business and here's why:

You will have hands-on operational training for 3 days. But, not just training on how to run the operations during an event, but business operation training as well.
It is a video game truck business after all so I did not want to leave out the business portion as many do. There is a training manual on the topic that we go over during training. Some elements in this book touch on the manual, but, unless the independent owner is part of the community it is not cheap to attain that knowledge.

Technical support on the phone with our head tech is available.
If there is a problem or an issue and you're not quite sure what to do, all you have to do is pick up the phone and our head technician will talk to you and help you troubleshoot the problem. There is not a single company that does something like that on the same level as *virtualrealitygametruck.com* . We go the extra mile because we want you to be successful.

By going with this hybrid model, you are invited to join a **Private *Mastermind Group.***
There is a very big difference between a mastermind group and sharing your thoughts and ideas through a blog

like platform. Let me elaborate on the difference.

A mastermind is a group of individuals doing something at a much higher level of execution where learning is key and results are the target.
In a discussion forum, besides throwing around words, very little actually gets done.
So how does this mastermind group work with virtualrealitygametruck.com? We, the independent business owners get together on a live video call or broadcast and troubleshoot, think and help each other succeed. This is done at least twice a month. We hold each other accountable and goals are set. By pushing ourselves as a collective we thrive on a winning mindset by manifesting real results through tactful action.

An 800 number for the first year of your operation is free and after that it's $15 a month. You are free to go with this option or not, it's completely up to you.
You do have the benefits of the mother like franchise website umbrella structure.
Basically, the main website, the home website is constantly worked on and invested in. So, you will feel the benefits from this even though you yourself will not be paying anything for the master website.

You are free and as a matter of fact even encouraged to do your own marketing as well outside of the http://www.virtualrealitygametruck.com website. When it comes to doing your independent marketing, we do not make any money from you helping you understand your local marketing.
Because we want you to succeed, when your phone is ringing with different marketers offering different

products, I am happy to personally jump on the phone call with you to find out more information and make sure that you do not over pay for a service that you may not need. In this day and age there are many fly by night marketing companies who present themselves as gurus. Be aware!

There are no franchise fees

There are no territory fees

There are no fees for the private Mastermind Group

There are no fees for consulting in local marketing

There are no fees for calling the technician on the phone to help you troubleshoot issues

To learn more or become a part of this business send inquiries to:

info@virtualrealitygametruck.com

3 GETTING STARTED

Chapter 3 is a short general outline for sequence of business execution steps: The full hands on training program is available through:
http://www.startavideogametruck.com

Free information is also available on the website above

Training Location: Los Angeles / Orange County CA

Okay let's say you are now at a point where you are about to get into the business, you need a little bit of guidance so that you make better decisions on your journey. Although this chapter does not cover everything in detail it does present elements that are taken from the training manual that we provide to all of our trainees when they are doing the hands-on program.

First you have to find out what type of vehicle you will be pulling your trailer with.

The way to determine what type of vehicle you need will be based on the terrain in which you operate. Common sense should dictate that if you are in a flat area you can get away with a smaller truck. However, if you are in an area that is full of mountains you definitely want a truck that is heavy-duty.

The next thing is figuring out what business system you will be going with. The previous chapter covered six of them. Which one works for you is something that you have to thoroughly think through. Then, you will need to purchase the trailer unit.

As you are doing your trailer shopping you need to figure out if you will be doing a DBA, LLC, or a corporation. The reason for "Doing Business As" or an LLC is so that you can establish a company business bank account, extra protection, and tie a merchant account to that business account. Without a merchant account, you will not be able to charge deposits for the events or be able to provide an option by which many pay for services rendered.

Having the proper insurance will determine if you can service parties that are in non-residential locations. Not having the proper insurance will directly block access to party venues.

Figuring out your market is another very important step. If you go to: http://www.startavideogametruckbusiness.com there is an episode that goes directly into how to generate business while you are waiting for your trailer to be built.

You will need to find a parking location if you cannot park the trailer and truck safely at your residence. In Los Angeles, we have a special location for our trailers. In this location, we have cameras, a big fence, and just in case, everything that moves also has a GPS. Any time one of our units move we can track it for safety reasons.

You should know the general policies and how to properly schedule the events.

Policies and scheduling is closely tied together. Your system needs to be smooth and accurate. Lack of organization when it comes to policies and scheduling will hurt you. ***"Be sure to spend enough time in figuring out what policies you need and the proper scheduling system that will work for you."***

Party preparation is a ritual that must be performed every single time before you head out to an event. Know what it is that you are doing before you go out to any event. There's a whole series of steps that is required to be performed prior to the event.

Research video games and systems that you will need. If you do not know what games are popular and what systems cater to different age groups you will put yourself at a disadvantage. Be sure to research and understand what systems and games work best in this business.

Maintenance is key for the longevity of the equipment. It's suggested that not only you find a good mechanic and trailer repair shop, but also that you learn how to do some basic things yourself. In the long run if you're running a one-man or a one-woman operation you will save money by doing basic maintenance yourself.

When you are on location at an event there is a sequence of steps that needs to be followed to properly and safely start the event. Be sure that you know what steps to take when you arrive to the event.

I know that many of you might be reading this and feeling a bit frustrated because even though a basic outline is presented to you, the fine details are missing. Like stated earlier, this chapter is nothing more than a general outline for sequence of business execution steps. The best way to know how to properly run the business is to go through the hands-on training by contacting us @:

http://www.startavideogametruckbusiness.com

4 ADD ON BUSINESSES

The beauty of operating a mobile video game truck business is that you can grow it while piggy backing other businesses from its marketing base. I would not suggest doing this until you can average **a minimum of 20 parties per month**. In one of my YouTube videos I mention that it is easier to get into a business that costs less money, however the competition will most likely be higher. The less it costs to start, the more competition you will encounter.

The video game truck business is not a low-ticket item and that is why you will not have as much competition as any of the add on businesses from this chapter. Therefore, by providing an amazing high-ticket product you can grow your services not by just expanding with more video game trucks but by adding different types of event service add-ons.

Photo booth business

Birthday characters' business

Laser tag business

Nerf business

Inflatable ball business

Catering business/ Taco man

Jumper business

DJ business

Choo-choo train business

Face painting business

Tent and chair rental business

The first business add on option is the **photo booth**.
In Los Angeles, my company has multiple photo booths operating. It works great as a dual business. The awesome thing about it is that it's very small and mobile. In my environment, it would be very difficult to operate a photo booth as a standalone business because there is way too much competition. Every student in school studding to become a photographer it seems like has a photo booth here. What they don't have is the marketing power of the video game truck.
The photo booth business provides an extra source of income that is highly profitable. Many times, the photo

booth can travel in the videogame trailer itself and it can be set up outside of the trailer at the event. If you have a 2.0 unit you can even put it inside the trailer. Also, because the learning curve for photo booth operation is low, it can function as a standalone business by itself. This is why I have the photo booth business as well.

If there are multiple events scheduled in one day, some could go specifically with just the photo booth and others with the video game truck.

Proper pricing of the photo booth and the video game truck combination will allow you to leverage both of the businesses by charging less for the photo booth than a competitor with still good profit.

If another photo booth company charges $400 for a three hour even, you can provide the same service for $275 alongside a full price charge of the video game truck. It makes a lot of sense for a party to rent both of these at the same time instead of going to two different companies and paying more.

The birthday character business is another interesting idea. I personally will not be dabbling in this business because it requires talent and talent management. Some costumes are very hot to wear so the employees or contractors who work with you or for you will need lots of breaks. Transportation also falls on the talent. The character business does have significant voids especially when it comes to princess parties. It is better to network than own this niche in my opinion.

Mobile laser tag
This is a very fun business but it cannot be operated in a busy city. In a state like California there are a million rules and regulations and liability insurance problems so it's

very difficult to do something like this in Los Angeles. However, if I was in a different state let's say like Texas or Nevada or Pennsylvania there's plenty of room to operate this fun business. I have seen this business in action and it makes sense financially if the marketing and territory of operations fits the demographics. You will need lots of room for this, literally.

The inflatable ball business
I am still monitoring this business to understand where it will be going. The problem with this business just like the laser tag business is that it requires lots of room. When I say problem, I mean problem for people like me who operate in Los Angeles. Maybe you are somewhere in Houston Texas or in a location that has lots of room. With room, this business will most likely be in your favor, considering that you can piggyback your marketing from the existing business of the video game truck.

Catering business or a Taco Man business
I would love to get into the catering taco man business and be able to set up the hot food right next to the video game truck. A very high percentage of people have catering come out to their events (primarily on Saturdays). While the video game truck is entertaining the kids in the front, the catering is in the back yard area.
This business like the birthday character business has lots of moving parts to it so be sure that you do your research and check the health and licensing standards. However, I will say that if you have a catering business and a video game truck business you can go into bigger venues and events. Events like ballgames, high school football games, etc. etc.

Jumper business

This business does not bring in as much revenue as a video game truck, not even close. The idea is very much hands-off after the delivery of the equipment followed by a simple pickup at the end of the day. If hypothetically let's say you are somewhere in Montana and there's not a single jumper or maybe just one jumper company in a 30-mile radius, then this business would be a no-brainer to add to the video game truck business. If you go to "the google" and 20 companies pop up in a 10 mile radius think twice before adding on this option.

DJ business

DJs are very popular if you are looking to break into a different type of market like weddings or something that caters to events where you are not directly going after the demographic of five to 12-year-old kids. Skill is required unless you hire someone.
If you do hire someone, be sure they know their craft. Be sure they are outgoing and with good energy.

The mobile choo-choo train

The choo-choo train business has little potential in my opinion and it is cumbersome. The fun aspect about this business is once you deliver it to a location it is very easy to operate. After the conductor hat is on, the function is to literally go in a little circle for 2 hrs and ring a bell. I think if you own a big entertainment company it will work for you.

Face painting business

Unless you are skilled in face painting you will need to hire someone else. Promoting this business is an option, especially to girl and prince's parties. Always a good idea to contract with someone on the side for face painting.

Doing it as an add on business that you own directly may not be as lucrative.

Tent and chair rental business
This is a very smart business if you are in an area where the population is not a small one. People always need to rent chairs, tables and tents. Especially for weddings and big gatherings. It is recommended you have a warehouse if you want to do it the right way because having a couple of chairs and tables is not enough. Contracting for big events opens many doors. This is a good big event business.

5 MARKETING 101

The foot work is key

Websites and SEO

Hounding the news

Facebook

Instagram

Yelp

Google PPC

Snapchat (indirect)

The Craigslist nono

The Groupn nono

The footwork is the key!
The second you open up your business you will have marketers try to contact you from every marketing platform available and sell you on all sorts of services. I remember when I started my phone was ringing day and night with people calling me from India, the Philippines, New York and many many other locations telling me that they were professional gurus and that they were going to help me. Do not fall for this. There is no such thing as the fast-easy solution to break through obscurity. The fastest way to get through obscurity is by doing the necessary foot work. In one of my YouTube videos, episode two, I provide a step-by-step guide as to what needs to be done while the trailer you ordered is in the construction phase. The beginning is always the most difficult part, but by following the directions you have a map. A person with a map in the forest can find a way out. You could be the smartest person in the world, without a map you will be lost. By watching episode two, you have that basic map outline. The next step is **to do the actual footwork.**
By reaching out and talking to schools, counties, communities, charities, fundraisers, churches etc. etc. You will begin to spread the word about what you are doing. You can beat anyone in your area of operations through over committed action. While others focus on online marketing you do both with a heavy human face to face element. Let me say that again, action is the key. The ability to make a spreadsheet, make the contacts and actually set up appointments to meet with people who make decisions will set you apart from everyone else. Always remember that you are in the human business. Meaning human communication and human contact. People are not necessarily lazy but to go out of their way to see something that you offer is not what most would

like to do. That is why if the mountain doesn't go to you, you need to go to the mountain. Step one is go to http://www.startavideogametruckbusiness.com and **watch episode two!**

Building your website and understanding search engine optimization

One of the biggest errors that you will possibly run into is believing that by creating an amazing flashing website your phone is going to ring and you're going to make a lot of progress with that website. There is something called search engine optimization when it comes to website work. In order for you to rank higher in search engine results the website will require a lot of optimization work, it has to also be full of quality content and you have to be very consistent. Any time I launch a website be it for one of my family member businesses or somebody else that I'm helping, I tell them the same thing. Your website will rank with proper work but do not expect it to rank anytime soon. Google places a new website in the sandbox stage in the beginning after it is launched. You have to look at a website as a long term factor. Yes it's very nice to have a website when you hand out your business card so people can go and find out more information, but if you're not willing to wait at least two years and commit to two years of work, strategically implementing tactics that will rank your website you are asking for something that will not happen. In the starting stage, while your website is under construction, you need to be doing the footwork and not focusing primarily on the website.

Hounding the news

A news source in your local community can provide much-needed leverage for you especially in the beginning. If nobody knows about you or your business, then your phone will not ring. So, I call this part "hounding the news". Basically, you find the local newspapers, the local news stations and radio stations and you keep contacting them as many times as it takes until you either get an interview or you are able to showcase your product. With local news, you can leverage a lot of media power and gain the necessary attention of people in your community. Hounding the news should be one of the top priorities when it comes to marketing especially when you are just starting out. One of the things I would suggest you do in this stage is make sure that you write out exactly what you want to say before you contact any news agencies. **If you sound like you know what you're talking about when contacting the news, your probability of getting an interview or showing your product is a lot higher**. For this part, you do need to have a basic website that can be used as a reference for the news contact person.

Facebook

I have tried doing many Facebook campaigns. It is a very strategic tool that I would suggest you outsource to a professional unless you want to commit the time to learning how to properly utilize Facebook. To be a practitioner of marketing on Facebook means that you know how to read demographics and how to properly connect to the people that make the decision. Facebook is a great place to brand market. Brand marketing takes time and effort. One thing that I tell all video game truck business owners is that if you do hire an SMM also known as social media marketing professional that you define from the start whether you're going after likes or if you're going after leads. Many times, kids out of college who look for jobs are not in full comprehension mode to what it actually means to run a business. Running a business means not just getting likes on Facebook and growing your brand, it also means generating money from leads. Don't get me wrong both are very important but in the beginning stage as you brand, you also need to make sure that if you hire someone who runs your Facebook campaign, that that person understands likes alone do not pay the bills.

Instagram
I love instagram. It caters much attention that is needed for your business. The indirect leveraging power of Instagram is effective. In general, you also have to understand what type of demographic uses this platform. Strategically implementing instagram could be of use but like Facebook do not chase the likes and followers unless branding is your number one priority.
Fighting for attention is a rough business. Instagram is an excellent indirect 3 second marketing tool.

Yelp
Yelp is a very interesting animal because in some parts of the nation it works wonders and in others it does absolutely nothing. When I think of Yelp I think of food, not a video game truck so I hope you can connect the dots here. Specifically looking at the demographics of yelp I can tell you that when it comes to the East Coast and West Coast cities Yelp is popular. As we narrow our search towards the middle of the country the power of Yelp is not as strong but it still works. If you want to try Yelp, do not be intimidated by the marketing tactics of Yelp sales

individuals. You have to understand them from their point of view. They want to do right by you and they want to generate business for themselves. I would suggest to give Yelp a try (especially if you are on the coast) but be stern on the phone. Business is not about chasing Yelp stars. There is much bias in reviews. If you serviced over 100 events and the first review was a one star because you showed up 10 minutes late and did not give a discount is not fair.
Why?
All because the parent had a bad day so they took out their rage on you?
Be careful.
Look at the patterns.
People give reviews if they are pissed off or very happy. If you are in San Francisco, Los Angeles, San Diego, New York or Miami go with Yelp and see how it delivers for you. I am sure your results will be much better than if you are in let's say Bismarck North Dakota. The best thing you can do is try it out and see if it works for you. Words of wisdom, focused results not stars is what should take priority.

Google pay per click
This is perhaps the most influential platform that you can use to get your name out. I love using Google pay per click, the only problem with it is that it is not a cheap tool to use. The cost of use will directly be reflected based on competition. As I am writing this, the cost per click in my area for one key term is $2.59 per click to drive business to my website.
Once you figure out your budget. I tell everyone that it's worth investing the time to learn how to Google Pay Per Click yourself versus hiring somebody else because you will pay a lot more if you hire someone in the beginning. If you

know that a click is roughly $2.50 to $3 dollars, you can question a so called "Professional" who is charging you $35 dollars for a conversion phone call if the data says the conversion cost is $12 dollars.
If this whole thing is going way over your head, you do need to be concerned. What you don't know will hurt you.

Snapchat

This is a new animal and I see a lot of people using it nowadays especially during events. One of the things that I found to be true which Snapchat, at least for this business, is that even though it is a very popular social tool for branding communication, as this book is being written, the majority of decision-makers are not on Snapchat yet. Let me elaborate. This unique platform is favored by the younger crowd. After doing your research you know that it is not the younger crowd but the parents who pay the bills. For example, like the Facebook crowd (The parent platform). Therefore, you can logically deduce that even though Snapchat is a supercool program to have and play with, investing too much time in Snapchat to convert a sale is not something that I would personally recommend at least right now for this business. Children do have leverage over parents and Snapchat will spark interest, but not the interest of the decision maker. Maybe I'm wrong but for me it has not produced the results that I wanted thus far.

The Craigslist no-no

If you are marketing on Craigslist in the beginning I can completely understand that you are trying to get into any platform where you can and break through obscurity. Do understand the following. Craigslist shoppers are a special type of individuals who will bargain for anything and everything. I love Craigslist, my entire family buys stuff from Craigslist. We bargain for everything if we need something from this platform. That is the type of mentality you will encounter if you advertise your product on Craigslist. If you are okay with bargaining, by all means use Craigslist and it might prove to be successful. In the beginning when I started I had a lot of business coming from Craigslist. However, Craigslist is the 80/20. What do I mean by that? 80% of your headaches will come from the Craigslist crowd. Once again maybe I'm wrong, by all means use it if it works for you.

I call it the Craigslist no-no because I do not like to bargain on the phone with someone who is trying to get the blockbuster deal of a lifetime. I am not a negotiating company that deals with different terms. In the next 5 plus years there will not be enough video game trucks to go around. It is a deficit. Following the basic economic market rules will help you in the long run. Dropping the price on Craigslist is a path to the dark side. Returning Craigslist customers, remember and re-quote the low prices from the past. "Always!"

The Groupon no-no
From experience, I will take the Craigslist marketing platform over the Groupon platform any day of the week and I am not a fan of marketing on Craigslist. I will leave it at that.

6 THE FUTURE OF THE BUSINESS

The Future of the Business

The future of this business has amazing potential. I believe that it has been firmly established that videogames are not going anywhere and that entertainment isn't going anywhere either. Briefly I've touched on the topic of convenience and how mobile service convenience is a major plus for this business. I personally believe that the future of the business is a very bright one and it is only the beginning as technology expands.

In order to continue to expand in this business, the 1.0 units can only go so far. It is the 2.0 unit that will take over due to the demand. I'm not telling everyone to get rid of their 1.0 units, however If you are already in the business, consider the fact that the ability to adapt is key. If you are operating in a very metropolitan area, adaptation for you will be crucial to succeed. Think of the virtual-reality wave that is about to hit from 2017 to 2025. If you have a 1.0

unit and next to you, you have a virtual-reality 2.0 unit that offers everything you offer plus virtual-reality, it will be difficult to outcompete.

I am well aware of the fact that VR units, primarily the headgear will become smaller over time, but not any time in the immediate future. The virtual-reality gaming is the next big thing and it's in the "original Mario Broz" stage right now. I do not mean to sound like a broken record but the 1.0 unit will not be able to keep up with the 2.0 unit. That is why, anyone who wishes to expand who is already in the business, needs to consider the elements of adapting to continue growth.

Growth, growth and more growth in this business.
I believe that over the next 10+ years this business will start filling in the final geographical gaps, the voids that are currently not filled. There are still more voids in servicing than there available operators doing the service. Only recently have the metropolitan areas have started to gain some traction but overwhelmingly as a whole the nation is still free for grabs. I am well aware of the fact that there are many naysayers who say that one cannot adapt this business at the speed of which the evolution of gaming is moving. However, I completely disagree with that. The niche business, once again as I said before, I will say it again, provides convenience. This is an amazing element that no other brick and mortar businesses can provide. **Entertaining a large group of kids at the convenience and location of the parents choosing.**

7
SOME QUESTIONS TO ASK BEFORE YOU BUY A USED UNIT

Buying a used unit is risky business. I have been there and I have done that. Personally, I will never do it again. But, that is my opinion. If you stumble on a great Craigslist deal, or a deal where someone is selling a used unit, consider -asking the following questions before you buy it.

Will you be rewrapping the outside? Or will you be taking over the company as a whole? Rewrapping of the trailer can cost up to 6 thousand dollars in some parts of the country. If it is a former franchise unit being sold, do you have permission to buy it as is?

Will you instantly get the pink slip?

What are the TV models? Are they older than 3 years and do they lack power efficiency? Any pixels or damage on the tvs?

What are the game system models, how old are they? How many games come with the unit? Do you have multiple copies of some games? Which ones? Why?

How old are the AC units? Have they been changed out? Year and make of Air conditioning units. Can freon be replaced in that model unit or does the whole unit need to be replaced?

Have the tires been changed?

What is the make of the generator?

How many hours are on the generator? If it's over 1,500 hours when was the last maintenance done on it?

Is there a gas tank underneath the trailer? Is it Compliant with local laws? Are there any scratches on the gas tank? How many hours can the generator run on a full tank at full capacity?

Have the seats ever been changed out?

Any rips in carpeting or seating?

Are there 4 remotes available per system? If no, why?

Is there an electrical front jack?

Is it leaf suspension? If yes, when were the springs changed last?

Is there an external power plug if the generator does not work?

Do you have the external plug adapter?

Are there 2 jack stands for stability for the rear?

What is the year and model of the trailer?

What is the weight of the trailer?

If all electrical and air-conditioning is turned on for 20 minutes on maximum will the generator shut down if you turn the AC units off and on again?

Does the generator take longer than 15 seconds to start?

Do you have a list of all clients previously serviced you can work off from, emails, names telephone numbers? (If taking over the area of service)

Are there any cosmetic or structural dents that are hidden under the wrap of the trailer?

Are the speakers wireless? If not, how are the audio cables routed? Check all sound bars for sound quality.

Are there any loose hinges on doors and cabinets?

Is the rubber lining on the doors still in place?

Are the U joints holding the leaf springs rusted?

Do you have a step latter?

Fire extinguisher?

Safety cones?

When were the brakes last changed?

Purchasing a proper truck for the used trailer unit will require proper attention. The truck needs to go through a full professional inspection. If it's a Ford, be sure the transmission is ok. If it is a smaller Avalanche model Chevy, be sure the breaks had an upgrade.

If the truck is sold as part of the deal, it is beneficial. However, remember the good saying "trust but verify" the purchase. If you are to operate the business in another area and you have a truck that is too big or small for your area of operations, it will hurt you.

If the trailer is older than 5 years I would not pay more than $30,000 and that's if it's in good condition along with a good tow vehicle. You will have more headaches with used stuff. BEEN THERE, DONE THAT.

Final word

I hope that some questions have been answered for you and that you have a better understanding of how the gears turn.

To purchase a 2.0 non-virtual reality unit that is designed to adapt to virtual reality please visit:
www.startavideogametruckbusiness.com

To purchase a 2.0 virtual reality unit and gain access to a private master mind community please visit
www.virtualrealitygametruck.com

You can contact me (Lee) directly at
info@virtualrealitygametruck.com

Lee Sulima

Photo booth add on to the business

Add a photo booth to the video game truck business

Full set up $3,500 When you purchase a standard 2.0 trailer Unit at regular price of $45,000

We build the photo booth for you!
Its brand new like the trailer.

The Video Game Truck Business: Is It For Me?

Basic Model Pictures

The Video Game Truck Business: Is It For Me?

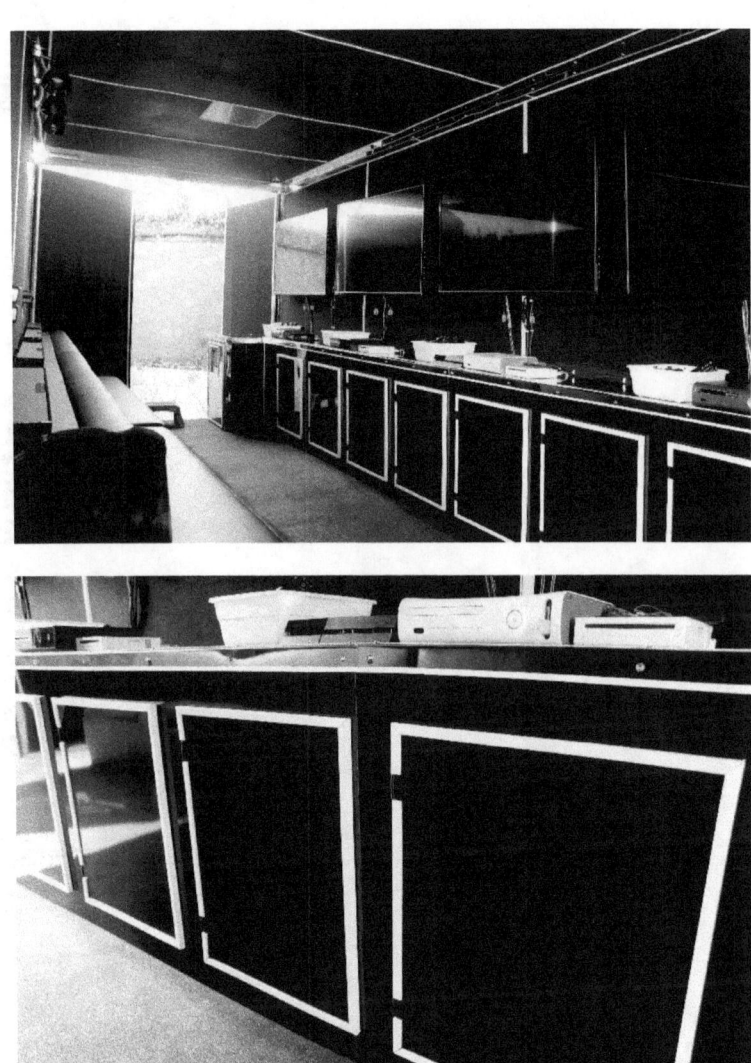

The Video Game Truck Business: Is It For Me?

The Video Game Truck Business: Is It For Me?

www.ingramcontent.com/pod-product-compliance
Lightning Source LLC
Chambersburg PA
CBHW061206180526
45170CB00002B/990